MW00425959

Study Guide to
East of Eden
by John Steinbeck

by Ray Moore

Revised Second Edition

Copyright 2019 Ray Moore

All rights reserved

Photo: John Steinbeck, 1962.
Photographer unknown.
Source: Nobel Foundation.

(This image is in the public domain
and so is not subject to copyright.)

Contents

East of Eden by John Steinbeck

Preface

A study guide is an *aid* to the close reading of a text, *never* a substitute for reading the text itself: a study guide aims to help the readers/students come up with their own interpretations of a text, not to provide ready-made interpretations to be accepted uncritically and absorbed.

This novel deserves to be read *reflectively*, and the aim of this guide is to facilitate such a reading. The Guiding Questions have *no* answers provided. This is a deliberate choice. The questions are for readers who want to come to *their own conclusions* about the text and not simply to be told what to think about it by someone else. Even 'suggested' answers would limit the *exploration of the text* by readers which is the primary aim of the guide.

In the classroom, I found that students frequently came up with answers that I had not even considered, and, not infrequently, that they expressed their ideas better than I could have done. Teachers do not need their own set of predetermined answers in order effectively to evaluate the responses of their students.

The notes I have provided briefly explain the most important historical and geographical references in the novel. The commentaries analyze the most significant points of each chapter. They do not set out to answer the questions, but sometimes they do cover the same ground. Each commentary represents my best understanding of a chapter at this point in time: they make no claim to be complete and certainly not to be definitive. Feel free to disagree.

Acknowledgements

As always, I am indebted to the work of numerous reviewers and critics. Where I am conscious of having taken an idea or a phrase from a particular author, I have cited the source in the text. Any failure to do so is an omission which I will immediately correct if it is drawn to my attention.

I believe that all quotations used fall under the definition of 'fair use.' If I am in error on any quotation, I will immediately correct it.

Thanks are due to my wife, Barbara, for reading the manuscript, for offering valuable suggestions, and for putting the text into the correct formats for publication. Any errors which remain are my own.

A Study Guide

Spoiler alert!

If you are reading the novel for the first time, you may wish to go straight to the Guiding Questions section and come back to the introductory sections later since they do explain everything that happens in the novel, including the ending!

Works Cited

SparkNotes Editors. "SparkNote on *East of Eden*." SparkNotes.com. SparkNotes LLC. 2003. Web. 11 May 2015.

TheBestNotes.com Staff. "TheBestNotes on *East of Eden*". TheBestNotes.com. 19 August 2014. Web. 26 May 2015.

East of Eden by John Steinbeck

Introduction

Plot Summary:

The novel traces the history of two families, the Hamiltons and the Trasks, over three generations. The Hamiltons come to the Salinas Valley, California, in the 1870s from Ireland. A few years later, Adam Trask brings his young wife Cathy to find a ranch in the valley having sold his half of the family's Connecticut farm to his brother Charles.

Steinbeck brings together the history of his mother's family (the Hamiltons) and the fictional story of the Trasks. The two families interact but also contrast. Each knows happiness and sorrow, but in the Trask family the myth of Cain and Abel seems to determine the relationships of first Adam and his brother Charles and then Aron and Cal, Adam's twin sons.

Central to the narrative is Cathy, the vicious young women who marries Adam, and later shoots him when he attempts to prevent her from walking out on him and her two sons. Not unreasonably, Adam tells his sons that their mother is dead, but in fact Cathy becomes the madam of a brothel in nearby Salinas, and it seems only a matter of time before the sons discover the lie that their father has told them…

Why Read this Book?

This is a long novel, and reading it requires a significant investment of time and effort. That said, it is for the most part a relatively easy read (the one exception being the discussions on the theological concept of *timshel*, though even these are pretty down to earth). Steinbeck himself called this novel "the big one," fully conscious that this would be his greatest achievement in the novel form, "I still think it is The Book, as far as I am concerned. Always before I held something back for later. Nothing is held back here. This is not practice for a future. This is what I have practiced for" (*Journal of a Novel*).

Literary critics tend to be rather patronizing about John Steinbeck. *East of Eden* was a best seller, but the reviewers were unenthusiastic. When Steinbeck was awarded the Nobel Prize in Literature for 1962, the howls of outrage from critics (led by *Time* magazine) were amazing (and, despite Steinbeck's outward dignity, very hurtful). Both the *Literary Companion to American Authors* and the *Bloom's Major Novelists* volumes dedicated to Steinbeck basically ignore what he wrote in the 1940s and 50s, and barely mention *East of Eden*. Readers, however, have

3

A Study Guide

long felt that this novel speaks to them of their own lives. Steinbeck died in 1968, but his books consistently continue to sell around two million copies a year. Certainly, the novel's theme and its positive (though complex) conclusion carry a message from which we can all benefit.

East of Eden could just be a forgotten classic waiting to be rediscovered!

Important: Issues with this Book.

There is virtually no bad language in this novel, no graphic violence, and no graphic sex. There *is* the fact that Cyrus Trask comes back from the Civil War with a sexually transmitted disease, and there is an account of the three whorehouses in Salinas at the turn of the century (one of which is run by Cathy). There are some examples of racial prejudice and of racist language (or at least of language that we find racist now), but even these are not extreme.

East of Eden by John Steinbeck

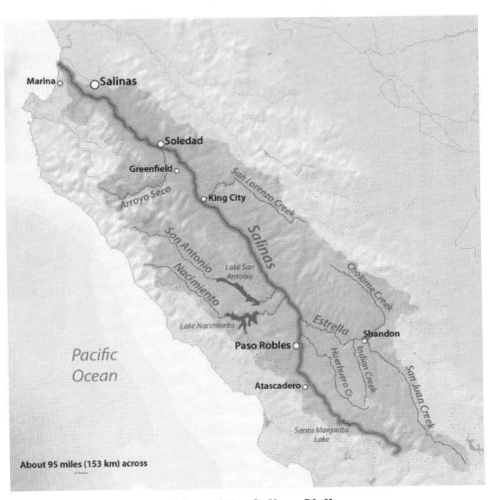

Map of the Salinas Valley

(Created from DEMIS Mapserver by Shannon1. This map is used under the ShareAlike 4.0 International License [CC BY-SA 4.0])

A Study Guide

Genre

The multi-generational family saga follows the lives of members of a single extended family or a number of interconnected families over several decades. This may be accomplished in a single novel (e.g., *Brideshead Revisited* by Evelyn Waugh, published in 1945) or in a series of novels (e.g. *The Forsyte Saga* by John Galsworthy, which occupies five books published between 1906 and 1921). The narrative normally begins several decades in the past and concludes close to the date of publication – very occasionally, the narrative goes beyond this date to some period in the future (e.g., *The Poisonwood Bible* by Barbara Kingsolver, published in 1998). The narrative includes the impact upon the different characters of actual historical events, of social change during the period of the narrative, and the resulting changing fortunes of the various characters.

Although it is a historical saga, *East of Eden* is more fundamentally a classic *Bildungsroman*, that is, a Coming of Age novel that tells the story (often, though not exclusively, in the first person) of the growing up of a young, intelligent, and sensitive person who goes in search of answers to life's questions (including the biggest question of all: Who they actually *are*) by gaining experience of the adult world from which they have been hitherto protected by their youth. The novel tells the story of the protagonist's adventures in the world and the inner, psychological turmoil in his/her growth and development as a human being. Examples include: *David Copperfield* (1850) and *Great Expectations* (1861) by Charles Dickens, *Sons and Lovers* (1913) by D. H. Lawrence, *A Portrait of the Artist as a Young Man* (1916) by James Joyce, *The Catcher in the Rye* (1951) by J. D. Salinger, etc., etc.

In *East of Eden* the reader watches Caleb struggle towards a real understanding of himself. Everything that comes before it really just provides the context for the presentation of Caleb's struggles to accept himself and the world as they are not as he would like them to be.

East of Eden is also an example of a *novel of ideas*, that is, a philosophical work which aims to communicate the author's ideas about moral and spiritual values. An inherent weakness in this genre is that the philosophy tends to be given primacy over the characters and the action both of which are frequently manipulated to illustrate the novelist's ideas. The author speaks (often at length) either in the voice of a narrator or through a sympathetic character. In *East of Eden*, the reader will find evidence of both first person musings (particularly in the ten interchapters

6

East of Eden by John Steinbeck

where the narrator addresses the reader directly) and of characters that embody a particular set of ideas and so lack the complexity of fully rounded characters. The main characters, however, are satisfyingly complex. Many critics argue that Steinbeck's need to vindicate his own understanding of the theological concept of *timshel* ('thou mayest') to guarantee human free will leads to tortured manipulation of characters and plot.

Need to Read background about Genesis

C & A

A Study Guide

Dramatis Personae - List of Characters

The following sketches help to identify the main characters.

The Hamilton Family:

Steinbeck draws on the history of his mother's family for these characters in the novel. The dates given are historical.

Samuel Hamilton (1831-1904) - Comes in 1870 to the Salinas Valley in California with his wife from the north of Ireland. He eventually owns 1,760 acres of marginal land in the barren hills east of King City. He is a very accomplished man when it comes to mending, improving, inventing, and making tools, but he never makes any money from his skills, because his futile attempts to secure patents for his many inventions eat up what little money he makes. He is a popular and well respected man who has a way of putting people at their ease.

Lisa Hamilton (1931-1918) - Samuel's wife is a dour Presbyterian. A tiny woman, she gives birth to four boys and five girls. Lisa has a powerful sense of the sinfulness of drinking alcohol, having fun and enjoyment, but she remains a sympathetic character because of her love for the members of her family.

George Hamilton - The eldest son of Samuel; "gentle and sweet," he grows into a "sinless man." However, he does not really figure in the narrative.

Will Hamilton (1864-1930) - The second son is practical and conservative. He becomes a car dealer and thus a wealthy and powerful man in the Salinas business community.

Tom Hamilton (1855-1912) - The third son becomes a rancher. Always a troubled man, he feels himself responsible for the death of his sister Dessie and kills himself out of guilt and grief.

Joe Hamilton - The youngest son is not cut out for farm work and attends Stanford College. He finds his niche in the new business of advertising in the East.

Lizzie Hamilton - The eldest daughter effectively leaves the Hamilton family and chooses instead to associate with her husband's family

Una Hamilton - The second daughter marries and moves to a remote area on the Oregon border where her life is poor and hard. Her death soon after

East of Eden by John Steinbeck

her marriage crushes Samuel's spirit and ages him considerably.

Dessie Hamilton (1857-1907) - The third daughter runs a dressmaking shop in Salinas. An unhappy love affair robs her of her vital happiness, and her business declines. She dies when Tom gives her salts to soothe her stomach, unintentionally aggravating her illness.

Olive (Ollie) Hamilton (1867-1934) - The fourth daughter becomes a teacher. Marries John Ernest Steinbeck and lives at 130 Central Avenue, Salinas.

Mollie Hamilton - The youngest daughter of Samuel and Liza. Mollie is the lovely one. She marries and moves to an apartment in San Francisco.

The narrator, John Steinbeck (1902-68) - The son of Olive Hamilton and John Ernest Steinbeck.

Mary (1905-65) - His younger sister. [Other sisters are not mentioned.]

The Trask Family:
Cyrus Trask (c. 1840-1894) - A farmer who serves as a private in a Connecticut regiment in 1862 during the Civil War. Having taken part in only one small engagement, he returns home with his right leg amputated at the knee and a virulent case of gonorrhea (*not* syphilis) caught from a black prostitute in the South. In later years he inflates his war service, obtains a powerful official position in Army administration, and moves to Washington. In the parallels with the *Genesis* story of Cain and Abel, Cyrus has the God role.

Cyrus' First Wife (c. 1840-1862) - A very religious lady who is infected with gonorrhea by her husband. She commits suicide out of a sense of sinfulness by drowning herself.

Alice Trask - She is seventeen when she becomes Cyrus' second wife. A very quiet, undemonstrative, withdrawn woman, she keeps the fact of her tuberculosis a secret from her husband.

Adam Trask (1862-1918) - Cyrus' only child by his first wife. He is a baby when his mother kills herself. In the parallels with the *Genesis* story of Cain and Abel, Adam has the Abel role.

Charles Trask (1863-1912) - Adam's half-brother, the son of Alice, is younger by a little over a year. He is a violent man who is deeply jealous of the fact that Cyrus appears to love Adam more. Charles plays the Cain role.

Aaron (Aron) Trask (1901-18) - The son of Adam and Cathy and twin brother of Cal. Aron plays the Abel role in the second generation of the Trask family.

Caleb (Cal) Trask (born 1901) - The son of Adam and Cathy and twin brother of Aron. Cal plays the Cain role, indirectly killing Aron by revealing that their mother is a prostitute, which leads Aron to join the army and die in World War I.

Lee (born c. 1880) - Adam Trask's long-serving Chinese cook and housekeeper who is both surrogate wife to Adam and surrogate mother to the twins. He is an educated and wise man who is a stabilizing and health-giving force in the Trask household.

Characters Connected with Prostitution:

Mr. Edwards - A man who, behind the cover of a respectable business in Boston, runs a prostitution ring, setting up women in small town hotels throughout Massachusetts and Connecticut and then rotating them every two weeks between towns. After employing Cathy as a prostitute, he falls in love with her, but on discovering that she is robbing him, he uncovers her involvement in the murder of her parents. He beats her nearly to death, and she crawls away to the nearest farm which is the one owned by Charles and Adam Trask.

Mrs. Edwards - His religious wife who chooses to remain ignorant of the nature of her husband's illegal activities.

Cathy (Catherine or Kate) **Ames** (1872-1918) - As a young girl, Cathy murders her parents by setting fire to their house and then commences a life of prostitution. She later marries Adam Trask who takes her from Connecticut to California despite her objections. Cathy subsequently becomes pregnant, gives birth, and shoots her husband when he tries to stop her leaving and abandoning her newborn twin sons. She returns to prostitution in Salinas. A manipulative, selfish, immoral woman.

Faye - The madam at the Salinas whorehouse where Cathy works as a prostitute. Faye comes to rely on Cathy, adopts as her daughter, and leaves everything to her in her will. Cathy slowly poisons her and, after Faye finally dies, takes over control of the brothel.

Ethel - A prostitute at Faye's brothel who obtains evidence that Cathy murdered Faye. Ethel tries to blackmail Cathy for a payment of $100 each month, but Cathy has her run out of town. She is later discovered to have drowned, though Cathy remains unaware of this.

Joe Valery - An escaped convict employed as 'muscle' at Cathy's brothel. As Cathy's health deteriorates, she comes to rely on Joe. He tries to trick Cathy by exploiting her fear of Ethel, but she learns of his betrayal and turns him in to the sheriff.

Rabbit Holman - A farmer from Salinas Valley who, being drunk, tells Cal about his mother's brothel and takes him there.

Minor Characters:

Abra Bacon - The daughter of the corrupt county supervisor in Salinas (the narrator implies that he steals money, or that he is one of the men whom Cathy blackmails, or both). Abra falls in love with Aron, but she shifts her affections to Cal and is one of the voices of wisdom that enables him to overcome his demons.

Louis Lippo - The farmer who introduces Adam Trask to Samuel Hamilton.

Horace Quinn - The sheriff of Monterey County from 1903 to 1919. He investigates the shooting of Adam Trask by Cathy and Cathy's own suicide.

Tom Meek - A constable in Salinas.

Julius Euskadi - A neighboring rancher, who attends the first meeting between Sheriff Quinn and Adam Trask after the shooting.

Dr. Wilde - The old doctor who Cathy manipulates in her plan to kill Faye.

Dr. Edwards and **Dr. Murphy** - Specialists in neurology who treat Adam after his final stroke.

Mr. Rolfe - The minister of Saint Paul's Episcopal Church in Salinas, who serves as Aaron's mentor. He is attracted to high church doctrines and inspires in Aaron a desire for purity.

Joe Fenchel - A German-American who is persecuted during the war by the citizens of Salinas because of his accent. The narrator remembers with shame how he and his sister participated in this persecution.

Alf Nichelson - A handyman in Salinas who knows all the gossip and tells Joe Valery the rumors about 'Kate' killing Faye.

East of Eden by John Steinbeck

Setting

The Connecticut farm on which Adam is raised is not a significant setting. It is the Salinas Valley that is the symbolic stage on which men engage in the eternal struggle between good and evil. Thus, though it is at times beautiful and bountiful, there are also times of drought and times of flood, there is rich land and there is poor land. The valley is bracketed by the "light gay" Gabilan Mountains "full of sun and loveliness" to the east, and the "dark and brooding" Santa Lucia Mountains to the west. It represents that land to the east of Eden where Adam and Eve went after their expulsion from the Garden of Eden.

A Study Guide

Structure of the Novel

A Tale of Two Families

The novel that became *East of Eden* began as a chronicle of the Hamiltons (Steinbeck's mother's family) written for his two sons. However, as the story progressed, more emphasis fell on the Trask family. It is the three-generational saga of the Trasks, in which the Cain and Abel story plays itself out twice, which gives the novel its moral theme and its structure: in a word, it is the core of the novel. The problem is that there are neither meaningful parallels nor meaningful contrasts between the stories of the two families which are "inextricably entangled" by events in the plot (Lisca). Thus, family history (in episodes like Olive Steinbeck's ride in an airplane) exists alongside, unrelated to, and often intruding upon the moral mythology explored in the history of the Trasks.

The Narrator

The narrator is named John, and his mother is Olive Hamilton, who married a man called Ernest John Steinbeck. The narrative refers to the Steinbeck house on the corner of Central Avenue and Stone Street, Salinas. (Incidentally, it is still there.) However, caution is needed. The narrator is a *fictionalized* version of the author, just as the story of the Hamilton family in the novel is fiction not history. The key difference is this: whilst the author *may* be all-knowing (omniscient), the narrator certainly is *not*. He says himself that he is having to reconstruct the past from "hearsay ... old photographs ... stories ... memories which are hazy and mixed with fable." Nowhere does he claim to understand everything about which he writes, though he does provide his own commentary on the story. In particular, the nature of the evil in Cathy remains a mystery to him - or rather, he changes and develops his understanding of it as the narrative progresses. All of this is a warning to the reader not to accept everything that the narrator says as intended by the author to be true.

Protagonists

There are two characters that may be identified as the protagonists of the novel: Adam Trask in the first generation and Caleb Trask in the second. Adam is a good son who respects, but does not love, his father. He is beset by the forces of evil, first in the form of a father who seems determined to mold his life, then by his brother, Charles, who being conscious of Cyrus' preference for Adam manipulates and hurts his brother, and finally by his wife, Cathy, who exploits, manipulates and

14

East of Eden by John Steinbeck

abuses his goodness. In turn, Cal feels himself to have 'the mark of Cain,' that is, to carry in his genes the evil of his mother. Cal suffers rejection by a father (ironically Adam) who wrongly prefers the apparent goodness of his other son, Aron, but he finally learns that he *can* choose goodness over evil; he is not a victim of his genes.

Antagonists

Several antagonists embody evil: Cyrus is a liar and thief who leaves Adam and Charles a fortune (the legacy of his corruption); Charles, who feels himself to be different from his good brother, thwarts Adam in life and leaves him the whole of his father's corrupt legacy; Adam becomes Cal's antagonist because he fails to see the good in him; but above all there is Cathy who is a force of evil in both her husband's life and her sons' lives (and the lives of everyone else whom she encounters). She appears from the start as an allegorical figure, a personification of evil to which the promise of *timshel* does not apply, but as we (and the narrator) eventually learn, she too has made her choice because, although from a child she saw signs of good and evil in people, she could never believe that the good was not merely a façade designed to hide, even to facilitate, their evil.

Climax and Resolution

The key climax of the plot occurs when, having failed to buy his father's love by a gift of money, Cal takes his revenge by showing Aron his mother's whorehouse. He does this to destroy the brother whom his father has always favored.

At the end of the novel goodness does *not* triumph over evil - that would be facile. Good is understood by the four main characters to *co-exist* with evil (Lee and Abra have known it all along, and Cal and Adam have had to learn it the hard way). This is the reality of the world in which man must live out his life and to evade that reality (as Adam once did and as Aron dies doing) is to be a coward. Cal discovers that he can forgive himself for his errors (terrible as they have been), and that he has freedom of choice in his life.

A Study Guide

Themes

Good versus Evil:

The narrator states that the conflict between good and evil is the basis of every good story ever written. (See Chapter 34.) On a superficial reading, the Cain and Abel story appears to divide men into the good (Abel) and the evil (Cain), and for two generations, the Trask family is divided between Cain and Abel figures (respectively Charles and Caleb, and Adam and Aron). Both Charles and Cathy have scars on their foreheads which represent 'the mark of Cain,' and these symbols appear to define them as evil. However, through the teachings of Lee, a deeper truth is found in the biblical story. Adam learns to forgive Cal the terrible thing that he did to his brother, and Cal learns that he is not inherently evil, that he has the freedom to choose goodness over evil, for man lives in a land to the east of Eden where perfection is impossible.

Cathy Ames represents the evil which certainly exists in the world. Steinbeck uses snake imagery to associate her with Satan: she is an Eve who has succumbed to evil without feeling the remorse of the biblical Eve. Increasingly, she retreats from the light into the darkness of her room and ultimately into the darkness of suicide. Cathy is the central character of the novel against which every other major character must test him or herself.

Free will and Determinism:

Determinism, the belief that the futures of men are entirely controlled by social, economic, even genetic forces beyond their power to control is not only represented in the novel by the Judeo-Christian concept of Original Sin, but also by the psychological and economic forces that determine the fate of individuals. As powerful as these forces are seen to be in the novel (indeed they destroy the lives of several characters), they are not presented as all-powerful. Just as man is not condemned by Original Sin, so he may live a fulfilled life no matter how lowly his place in society. (Samuel and Lee are the prime examples.)

Parenting

The novel is full of examples of really bad parenting. Both Cyrus and Adam show an unfair preference for the son they conceive to be 'good,' and in doing so seek to mold that son in their own image (Cyrus by forcing Adam into the cavalry and Adam by insisting that Aron must go to college). Nothing the rejected child can do appears able to win back their father's love (Cyrus does not value Charles' gift of an expensive knife, and Adam rejects Cal's gift of money). Abra's parents want her to be a stereotypical wife and mother, married (of course) to someone rich and socially acceptable.

In contrast, Samuel and Liza bring up a family in which individuals are free to find themselves. Some prosper and some end tragically; some are happy and others are sad; but they all control their own fates. Ironically, Lee is the best parent in the whole novel. He is the surrogate wife of Adam and mother to the twins. In this role, he provides the wisdom, understanding, and love that allows the Trask family to break out of the vicious cycle of bad parenting.

Inheritance

Several characters leave money (lots of money) in their wills: Cyrus leaves his ill-gotten fortune equally to his two boys, Adam and Charles; Charles leaves his untouched portion equally to Adam and Cathy; Cathy leaves her fortune exclusively to Aron, but he will never collect it because he dies. In each case, the money seems like a curse passed from one generation to the next and it parallels, and perhaps symbolizes, the idea of genetic inheritance. Cyrus dislikes Charles because he sees in the boy his own tendency to evil; Adam prefers Aron because he is the twin who seems most like himself; Cal fears that he has inherited Cathy's evil; Cathy seeks to infect Aron with her own evil in her will.

Both forms of inheritance come to an end in the resolution of the novel. Adam has lost in his lettuce scheme all of the tainted money that he inherits; Cal burns the tainted money he makes profiteering during the war; Cathy's fortune is left to a dead man. Similarly, by blessing his son Cal, Adam recognizes that he has not genetically inherited his mother's propensity for evil.

All-in-all, Steinbeck does not have much time for money. The admirable characters in the novel (like Samuel and Lee) either have very little or have made what little they have by their own honest, hard work. Even those Hamiltons who are successful in business are presented less sympathetically than those who remain relatively poor. Steinbeck emerges as deeply suspicious of the modern age.

The Passage of Time

Any multi-generational saga must also be the story of the changing times. This novel takes us from the Civil War, through the final years of the American West and the settlement and development of the Salinas

Valley, to the modern world of cars, airplanes and the First World War. The values of the past are represented in the character of Samuel Hamilton, who embodies the ingenuity, philosophy, optimism, and warm spirit of the pioneer age, and the future is represented by those of his children who pursue their interest in business and in the advances of technology. The narrator does not always represent change as progress, and there is certainly some nostalgia for the past, mainly agrarian, times. However, this is a story about living in the world that *is* and not in the world as we should like it to be: Cal has within him the potential to reconcile earlier values with the modern world.

Racism

Steinbeck was an outspoken opponent of racism all of his life. (You really should get hold of a copy of *Travels with Charley* and read the chapter on his experience of the extreme racism he encountered in the South during the Civil Rights Era. It is very moving.) Lee is subject to racial stereotyping throughout the novel even by people (like Adam's nurse) who are in every other way pleasant. With people other than those whom he trusts, Lee copes with prejudice by playing the stereotype Chinaman and speaking in pigeon-English. The irony, of course, is that he was born in America.

Racism against Germans flairs up during The Great War, and the narrator shamefully (but honestly) tells the story of the part that he and his sister played in baiting the one supposed German in Salinas, Mr. Fenchel a patriotic and inoffensive tailor.

East of Eden by John Steinbeck

Study Guide Questions

The commentaries provide an introduction to thinking about each chapter and the occasional notes should explain any obscure references.

The questions are designed to help you to locate and to understand characters, plot, settings, and themes in the text. They do not normally have simple answers, nor is there always one answer. Consider a range of possible interpretations - preferably by discussing the questions with others. Disagreement is to be encouraged!

Part One

Chapter 1.

[Section 1] The novel opens with first person narrative. The speaker recalls his childhood in the Salinas Valley and particularly his experience of the natural world of the valley. He then places that experience into a longer perspective, recalling the experiences of his father and his grandfather. These, in turn, are placed in geological time as he describes the changes in sea level and the impact they had on the landscape of the valley. The valley emerges as a living being in metaphors such as "[t]he river tore the edges of the farm lands" and "the land would shout with grass." Steinbeck sets up the biblical metaphor of good versus evil (light versus dark), the former being represented by Gabilan Mountains, to the east, and the latter by the Santa Lucia Mountains to the West. Between these two mountain ranges, the narrative of the Hamilton and Trask families will play out.

[Section 2] A brief history of human occupation follows tracing the occupation of the valley by Native Americans, Spaniards and finally Americans. The natives were indolent; the Spanish were greedy for land and wealth; and the Americans appeared to have an insatiable lust for owning land, even if it was worthless.

Questions

1. A central theme of the chapter is the opposition of good and evil. Explain how this theme is developed in the descriptions of: the mountains to the east and to the west of the valley, the changing nature of the Salinas River in wet and dry months, and the different effects of abundant water and drought on farming.

Chapter 2.

[1] The narrator details the arrival in the valley of the narrator's maternal

grandfather, Samuel Hamilton, whose homestead is on barren, marginal land because he is poor. Samuel becomes a blacksmith and well-digger; he also offers help to sick and pregnant humans and animals.

[2] The narrator introduces Adam Trask, a rich man who, some years later, comes to the valley and purchases good land.

Notes:

Dr. Gunn's Family Medicine - "This popular home medical guide by Dr. John C. Gunn (ca. 1795-1863) was first published in Knoxville in 1830 ... Designed to serve as a guide for frontier and rural families who lived great distances from even primitive medical care, the book covered virtually any possible miscarriage of health. It contained extensive references from the works of the major medical men and journals of the time, making it also a useful textbook for largely self-taught doctors in all rural areas." (*The Tennessee Encyclopedia of History and Culture*)

Questions

2. The dominant opinion is that men at this time were able to survive and even flourish on poor land because of their faith in God. What alternative view does the narrator favor?

Chapter 3.

[1] Tells the story of Adam Trask's father, Cyrus, a Connecticut farmer, and his two wives. Cyrus enlists in the Union Army in June 1862, but he is a fraud: a soldier who sees almost no action before he is wounded but who, in later years, gives the impression of having been an expert of military strategy and present at every major battle of the war. Upon his return, Cyrus infects his wife with the clap, and, being a very religious woman, she decides to kill herself. She writes a suicide note confessing to sins she never committed, wraps herself in a shroud, and drowns herself in a shallow pond.

[2] Adam and Charles grow up to be very different: Adam is quiet and intellectual, while Charles is physically active and confident in his abilities. Adam is drawn to his step-mother, Alice, when he sees her secretly smiling when she thinks that she is alone and unseen. He secretly leaves her little gifts to encourage her to smile - a sign of his goodness.

[3] The differences between Adam and Charles become more pronounced: Charles cannot accept ever being outperformed by his elder brother. Cyrus confides in Adam that he has been pushing him so hard because he senses a weakness in him and because he loves him better than he loves Charles.

[4] Charles is resentful about Cyrus's recent birthday: Charles saved his money and bought him an expensive German knife, but Cyrus seemed indifferent to the gift, yet deeply appreciative of the stray puppy that Adam gave him. Suspecting that their father loves Adam but does not love him, Charles attacks Adam violently and might have killed him if Adam had not hid in a drainage ditch. Ironically, Alice defends Charles even as she tends Adam's wounds: the little gifts that Adam has been secretly giving her, she believes to have come from Charles.

Certain themes are <u>foreshadowed</u> here that will be important in the story of the next generation:

- the dominant father who molds his sons in his own image;
- the son who sees through his father's bluster and façade of confidence;
- a father's preferential love for one of his two sons;
- two mismatched brothers (recalling the biblical story of Cain and Abel);
- mistaken love.

Notes:

Grand Army of the Republic - The G.A.R. was established April 6th, 1866, and by 1890 it numbered 409,489 men, all of whom were honorably discharged Union veterans of the "War of the Rebellion" (i.e., they had served between April 12, 1861 and April 9, 1865).

Questions

3. Read the story of Cain and Abel as it appears in *Genesis* Chapter 4, Verses 1-17 (*KJV*):

And Adam knew Eve his wife; and she conceived, and bare Cain, and said, I have gotten a man from the LORD. And she again bare his brother Abel. And Abel was a keeper of sheep, but Cain was a tiller of the ground. And in process of time it came to pass, that Cain brought of the fruit of the ground an offering unto the LORD. And Abel, he also brought of the firstlings of his flock and of the fat thereof. And the LORD had respect unto Abel and to his offering: But unto Cain and to his offering he had not respect. And Cain was very wroth, and his countenance fell. And the LORD said unto Cain, Why art thou wroth? and why is thy countenance fallen? If thou doest well, shalt thou not be accepted? and if thou doest not well, sin lieth at the door. And unto thee shall be his desire, and thou shalt rule over him. And Cain talked with Abel his brother: and it came to pass, when they were in the field, that Cain rose up against Abel his brother, and slew him. And the LORD said unto Cain, Where is Abel thy brother? And he said, I know not: Am I my brother's keeper? And he said, What hast thou done? the voice of thy brother's blood crieth unto me from the ground. And now art thou cursed from the earth, which hath opened her mouth to receive thy brother's blood from thy hand; When thou tillest the ground, it shall not henceforth yield unto thee her strength; a fugitive and a vagabond shalt thou be in the earth. And Cain said unto the LORD, My punishment is greater than I can bear. Behold, thou hast driven me out this day from the face of the earth; and from thy face shall I be hid; and I shall be a fugitive and a vagabond in the earth; and it shall come to pass, that every one that findeth me shall slay me. And the LORD said unto him, Therefore whosoever slayeth Cain, vengeance shall be taken on him sevenfold. And the LORD set a mark upon Cain, lest any finding him should kill him. And Cain went out from the presence of the LORD, and dwelt in the land of Nod, *on the east of Eden.* And Cain knew his wife; and she conceived, and bare Enoch: and he builded a city, and called the name of the city, after the name of his son, Enoch. (*King James Version,* emphasis added)

Make a list of the similarities you find between this and the story of Adam and Charles.

Chapter 4.

[1] That night, Charles evades Cyrus who has gone looking for him with a shotgun. He stays away from home for two weeks, by which time Adam has been inducted into the cavalry.

[2] While he is away, Adam receives detailed, self-revelatory letters from Charles in which he talks of his deepest fears such as his impression that the family home is in some way haunted. Alice finally dies of tuberculosis, and Cyrus is given a prestigious job in Washington.

Chapter 5.

[1] At first, people in the valley are suspicious of Samuel's ideas and his reading of books, but they eventually take to him. Just as Samuel is continually adding lean-tos to the family home, so nine children are born, all different, yet somehow they form "a well-balanced family" of which Samuel is justly proud.

Questions

4. The Hamilton and Trask families are very different. The tone is set by

the two family patriarchs: Samuel and Cyrus. Compare and contrast the characters of these two men.

Chapter 6.

[1] Charles works alone on the farm for several years. As a result of an accident, he has a dark scar on his forehead which bothers him greatly. He writes to Adam, "It just seems like I was marked."

[2] In 1885, after serving for five years, Adam is discharged, but unable to face returning home he reenlists. His father uses influence to have Adam assigned to Washington where Cyrus is a great and important man in the War Department. Adam refuses the offer of admission to West Point.

[3] Alone on the farm, Charles is lonely and unhappy, but he manages the farm well and it prospers. He does not spend any of his inheritance.

Chapter 7.

[1] Adam serves five more years in the cavalry which he leaves in late 1890 with the rank of sergeant. For three years, he becomes a hobo spending the final year working on a prison chain-gang in Florida. Finally he escapes and makes his way home to Connecticut.

[2] Meanwhile, in February 1894, Charles has received news of Cyrus' death, his lavish funeral, and a joint inheritance of $103,000.

[3] Adam returns to the Connecticut farm. Charles shares with Adam his suspicion that their father became rich dishonestly and that his war stories were false. Because he loved his father, Charles is devastated by this possibility, while Adam chooses not to believe his father was ever dishonest.

Notes:

I.W.W. - The Industrial Workers of the World (the "Wobblies") is an international, radical labor union formed in 1905. From the start the organization welcomed all social classes, races and occupations unlike other labor unions which existed to support specific types of working people. It was seen by its opponents as a socialist and anarchist group which set out to destroy the wage system by direct action. Its supporters see it as a genuinely progressive organization working for a more equitable society.

Questions

5. How has the balance of power between Adam and Charles shifted?

6. Why does Charles doubt his father's honesty, when, in the face of the

same evidence (Cyrus' official papers) Adam does not? How is this issue related to the question of why Cyrus insisted on sending Adam into the Army but did not feel the need to do the same with Charles?

7. The story of Adam and Eve is told in Genesis Chapters 2 and 3. Here is an edited version:

And the LORD God took the man, and put him into the garden of Eden to dress it and to keep it. And the LORD God commanded the man, saying, Of every tree of the garden thou mayest freely eat: But of the tree of the knowledge of good and evil, thou shalt not eat of it: for in the day that thou eatest thereof thou shalt surely die ... And they were both naked, the man and his wife, and were not ashamed. Now the serpent was more subtil than any beast of the field which the LORD God had made. And he said unto the woman, Yea, hath God said, Ye shall not eat of every tree of the garden? ... And when the woman saw that the tree was good for food, and that it was pleasant to the eyes, and a tree to be desired to make one wise, she took of the fruit thereof, and did eat, and gave also unto her husband with her; and he did eat. And the eyes of them both were opened, and they knew that they were naked; and they sewed fig leaves together, and made themselves aprons ... And the man said, The woman whom thou gavest to be with me, she gave me of the tree, and I did eat. And the LORD God said unto the woman, What is this that thou hast done? And the woman said, The serpent beguiled me, and I did eat ... Unto the woman he said, I will greatly multiply thy sorrow and thy conception; in sorrow thou shalt bring forth children; and thy desire shall be to thy husband, and he shall rule over thee ... And the LORD God said, Behold, the man is become as one of us, to know good and evil: and now, lest he put forth his hand, and take also of the tree of life, and eat, and live for ever: ... So he drove out the man; and he placed at the east of the garden of Eden Cherubims, and a flaming sword which turned every way, to keep the way of the tree of life. (*KJV*)

What similarities do you find between the story of original sin and Cyrus' lies and dishonesty?

Chapter 8.

[1] Cathy Ames is born in a town in Massachusetts. From birth, she appears entirely without a moral conscience.

[2] At the age of ten, her mother finds Cathy engaged in sex-play with two boys in the barn, but Cathy manages to cast all blame on the boys. Only

her father has doubts about her innocence and a growing suspicion that the valuables she claims to 'find' are actually stolen.

[3] When Cathy is fourteen, a teacher at her school with whom she has had some sort of relationship mysteriously commits suicide.

[4] One day soon after she turns sixteen, Cathy refuses to go to school. She runs away to Boston, but is brought back by her father and whipped.

[5-6] Cathy gives every appearance of having learned obedience, but she formulates a plan to burn down the family home, kill her parents, steal the wages from the family business, and fake her own murder. The plan works perfectly.

Questions

8. Speaking of the actions of Shakespeare's Iago (Othello), the critic Coleridge used the term "motiveless malignity" - it fits Cathy rather well. She appears to be an embodiment of pure evil: she is manipulative and totally selfish. If the Hamiltons' future appears to be determined by their poverty, and the Trasks' future by the 'curse' of Cyrus' dishonesty, Cathy's future seems to be biologically determined. How convincing do you find the presentation of Cathy's character?

Chapter 9.

[1] Behind the cover of being a businessman, Mr. Edwards runs an extensive prostitution ring in the small towns around Boston. Several years after killing her parents, using the name Catherine Amesbury, Cathy comes to him ostensibly looking for work as a prostitute and becomes his kept mistress. For the first time he has fallen in love with a whore.

[2] Their relationship goes smoothly until Mr. Edwards insists on Cathy drinking champagne when she gets drunk and tells him how she really feels about him.

[3] Apparently contrite, Cathy resumes the relationship, but when Edwards discovers her to be stealing from him he looks into her past and discovers the truth. He takes her back to her hometown and beats her, leaving her for dead.

Questions

9. The chapter ends, "[Cathy] turned in at a gate and almost made the steps of the house before she fainted." What can you predict about the plot of the novel?

Chapter 10.

[1] Adam and Charles live together on the farm until both are in their late

thirties. Every so often tensions between them erupt and Adam leaves for a while.

[2] Returning from his first such absence, Adam broaches the subject of moving to California.

[3] After a trip to South America, Adam returns again. Charles is impressed when Adam finally tells him of his year as a prisoner in Florida. Charles has always thought of Adam as wholly good.

Questions

10. Explain the different reaction that the two brothers have to the prospect of living on the farm for the rest of their lives? How does this show the fundamental difference between the two men?

Chapter 11.

[1] Adam and Charles hear Cathy crawling onto the porch. Despite Charles' objections Adam insists on taking her in and sends his brother for the doctor.

[2] The doctor attends to Cathy's serious injuries and tells Adam that he will have to inform the sheriff. Charles continues to oppose Adam's wish to keep Cathy at the house. When the sheriff questions her, Cathy feigns amnesia.

[3] Charles tells Cathy that he does not trust her and will turn her out as soon as she is able to walk. He convinces her that she said something incriminating about her past in her sleep.

[4] Adam asks Cathy to marry him. Knowing that she needs protection, she has already decided to accept, but asks him for time to consider. She also asks him not to tell Charles.

[5] Adam takes Cathy into town and marries her. On their wedding night, she gives him a sleeping draft and sleeps with Charles.

Questions

11. As Adam tends to Cathy's wounds, he remembers his stepmother standing nursing him after he was beaten by Charles. How does this explain Adam's determination to look after Cathy?

12. Charles tells Cathy that when he looks at her, "'There's something - I almost recognize.'" Explain the psychological and the physical (symbolic) similarities between the two.

13. Why do you think that Cathy sleeps with Charles on her wedding night? The BestNotes author perceptively comments, "Having sex with Charles on her wedding night to Adam indicates that Cathy symbolically married Charles while she literally married his brother." Explain what you

think is meant by this.

A Study Guide

Part Two

Chapter 12.

The nineteenth century gives way to the twentieth. For some men it is the loss of a better way of life and for others it is the chance for society to begin anew.

Notes:

Reference is made to the War of 1812-5 between Britain and the U.S.A. during which Washington was attacked and the White House burned down, and to the war of 1846-8 between Mexico and the U.S.A. by which the latter gained a great deal of territory.

Questions

14. What is the narrator's own considered view of the nineteenth century?

Chapter 13.

[1] The narrator believes that individuals, not groups, have great ideas and perform great deeds. He worries that the move toward collectivism in modern society will kill human creativity. His faith in the "free exploring mind of the individual human" implies a belief in free will that will be important in the novel.

[2] Adam sells his half of the farm to Charles, takes the reluctant Cathy to California, and looks for properties in the Salinas Valley. Finding herself to be pregnant, Cathy attempts to abort the fetus and nearly dies due to loss of blood. She lies to the doctor about her fear that her baby will inherit the family epilepsy, and he does not tell Adam what she has done. Adam is considering buying the prosperous Bordinis ranch.

[3] Anxious to find out about water on the property he is considering, Adam visits Samuel Hamilton for the first time. Samuel describes the paradoxical nature of the valley: it is a good place to raise a family but also, "'There's a black violence on this valley.'" Adam resolves to buy the Bordinis ranch.

Notes:

The Swede referred to is Alfred Nobel (1833-96) who invented dynamite in 1866. In his 1895 will he set aside the bulk of his estate to establish the Nobel Prizes, to be awarded annually without distinction of nationality.

Questions

15. Explain why it is that Adam is so blind to the reality of his wife's character.

16. What is it that Samuel says about the dual nature of the Salinas Valley (its light and dark sides)?

Chapter 14.
[1] Olive Hamilton (the narrator's mother) spends several years as a school teacher at Peach Tree before marrying.
[2] During the Great War, Olive excels at selling war bonds. To mark her achievement, she is given a flight in an Army plane.

Notes:
Liberty Bonds "were first utilized during the first World War to support the allied cause in World War I. Subscribing to the bonds became a symbol of patriotic duty in the United States and introduced the idea of financial securities to many citizens for the first time. This allowed private citizens to purchase a bond to help support the military effort. After the war, the bond could be redeemed for its purchase price plus interest." (LibertyBonds.com)
In World War I aerial combat, an Immelmann turn (named after the German air ace Max Immelmann who first developed it) was a maneuver involving rolling and looping the airplane so that it could turn back on its path to renew its attack on an enemy plane.

Questions
17. This chapter on Olive is designed to contrast the presentation of Cathy in the previous chapter. What key differences between the two are stressed?

Chapter 15.
[1] Adam begins rebuilding the ranch he has bought sparing no expense. It is a place where he intends to found a dynasty.
[2] Adam sends his newly hired Chinese servant, Lee, to fetch Samuel to discuss drilling wells on his land.
[3] Samuel accompanies Adam around his land locating places to drill wells. Adam tells Samuel how his life changed when he met Cathy and of his dreams of building a beautiful garden, an Eden, for his wife and family. Samuel wants to tell him he is living in a fantasy world.
[4] At dinner, Samuel senses that something is wrong with Cathy, but he does not know what it is.
[5] Left alone, Cathy tells Adam that she will leave the ranch as soon as she can after the baby is born, but he does not take her seriously.

A Study Guide

Notes:

"Othello's handkerchief" - In the play of the same name, Othello gives his wife, Desdemona, a handkerchief as a gift. She loses it, and it is used by Iago to convince her husband of her adultery. Samuel is saying that he should show Adam that basing his happiness on Cathy is an unreal illusion.

Questions

18. Why does Cathy feel uncomfortable with the servant Lee? What similarities, and what differences, do you find between the way that Lee and Cathy present themselves to other people in order to ensure their own survival?

19. Adam tells Samuel of his dream of building "'a garden of my land. Remember my name is Adam.'" Samuel's reaction is to say, "'It's my duty to take this thing of yours and kick it in the face ...'" Adam does not understand what Samuel means by this speech. Can you explain?

Chapter 16.

[1] As Samuel rides home in the dark of evening he puzzles over what it is about Cathy that disturbs him and decides that it is her eyes: they have in them no humanity, like the eyes of a criminal he once saw who was about to be hanged.

[2] The following morning, Samuel describes his experience to his wife Liza and begins to prepare for a winter of work on Adam's ranch.

Questions

20. During Samuel's ride home, we are told that he "brooded over his own healed loss." To what do you think this refers?

Chapter 17.

[1] The narrator questions whether Cathy was actually a monster. Perhaps it was just that no one understood her motivations.

[2] Drilling a well on Adam's property, Samuel strikes a meteorite. Lee arrives with the news that Cathy has gone into labor.

[3] Samuel helps Cathy as best he can. At one point, she viciously bites his hand. Two non-identical twins are born, but Cathy refuses to see them. Samuel sends for his wife.

[4] Liza stays with the Trasks for a week and then returns home.

[5] Cathy plans her escape by ensuring that no one is at the ranch except Adam and herself. When he tries to stop her, she shoots him in the shoulder.

East of Eden by John Steinbeck

Questions

21. When it comes to every major character except Cathy, the <u>narrative</u> is <u>third person omniscient</u>. Explain what this means. With Cathy, the narrative is <u>third person limited</u>. Explain what this means.

Chapter 18.

[1] Deputy Horace Quinn questions Adam about how he was shot. Adam insists that the shooting was an accident; he says that his wife left and he does not know why.

[2] Quinn goes to Salinas to ask the advice of the sheriff. He learns that the new girl at Faye's whorehouse fits Cathy's description. The sheriff urges Quinn to say nothing about it to anyone.

[3] Adam has given up on life, but Samuel advises him to go through the motions of living.

Questions

22. How does the sheriff justify his laissez-faire attitude to the three brothels in Salinas?

Chapter 19.

[1] The narrator explains the position of the whorehouse in Western culture and describes the three brothels in Salinas.

[2] Cathy (calling herself Kate Albey) quickly settles in at Faye's making herself popular with the other girls and works very hard to win Faye's approval.

[3] Cathy recalls a visit from the sheriff shortly after she came to Faye's. He had told her that he knew who she was and that she had shot Adam. He had also told her that he would take no action provided she caused no trouble.

[4] Cathy becomes increasingly indispensable to Faye herself.

Notes:

"Pinkham" - Lydia Estes Pinkham (1819 - 83) invented *Vegetable Compound* an herbal-alcoholic "women's tonic" to relieve menstrual and menopausal pains. In an age when many patent medicines were dangerous 'snake oil,' Pinkham's actually seems to have been effective.

Chapter 20.

[1] Faye calls Cathy her daughter and suggests that she give up working as a whore and help Faye manage the brothel. Faye tells her to come to her room in the afternoon for a surprise. Cathy begins spreading a rumor that

Faye is not well.

[2] Cathy goes into Faye's room. Faye shows her a new will that she has written in which everything is left to Cathy on her death. Faye insists that they drink wine to celebrate, and (just as she did with Mr. Edwards) Cathy loses control and says some terrible things about how she really feels about Faye.

[3] When she is sober, Cathy evaluates the situation. With care she arranges everything so that she can convince Faye that what happened was only a terrible nightmare. In this she is successful.

Notes:

The Woodmen of the World, founded in 1890, was (and still is) a fraternity formed to ensure the financial security of its members through mutual insurance.

Questions

23. Look up the word "sadomasochism." Explain how it describes the kind of sex that Cathy offers her clients and how it explains her cruelties to her parents, to Adam and to Faye.

Chapter 21.

[1] Cathy manipulates things so that the existence of the will becomes public knowledge in the brothel. She feigns illness to see Dr. Wild, but refuses to have him called out to the whorehouse.

[2] In the doctor's surgery she steals some poison.

[3] Faye talks to Cathy about the two of them going to Europe the following summer, and Cathy feels she has to pretend to be delighted.

[4] Cathy begins to poison Faye, taking care that no suspicion falls on her by appearing to be Faye's dedicated nurse. When Faye dies, Cathy is apparently inconsolable.

Notes:

Croton oil is poisonous though it has uses in medicine. It is a purgative: even in the smallest amounts, it causes diarrhea. Cascara Sagrada is also a laxative used to treat constipation.

Questions

24. Many critics see Steinbeck's depiction of Cathy's character as the novel's major flaw. The problem is that the narrator claims not to be able to understand her evil and can only fall back on the idea that she was born evil. As a result, the reader never learns about her motivation. To what extent do you agree with this line of criticism?

East of Eden by John Steinbeck

Chapter 22.

[1] Fifteen months after Cathy left him, Adam is still barely living. The ranch is unattended and he takes little notice of his twins who remain unnamed.

[2] When Samuel learns about this from Lee, he determines to go to the Trask place and shake Adam out of his lethargy.

[3] Samuel confronts Adam and strikes him twice; it is the only way he can think to bring Adam back to himself and it works. For the first time, Adam realizes how different his two sons are. He worries about the "blood" they may have inherited from Cathy.

[4] Over dinner, Adam, Samuel and Lee set about naming the twins. There is an extended discussion of the story of Cain and Abel. Finally it is decided that the "'smart ... dark one'" will be called Caleb and the other Aaron. There is foreshadowing that Caleb (like Charles and Cathy) will bear the mark of Cain, while Aaron will be Abel, a dutiful sun, like his father. [Note: As a young boy, Aaron finds the biblical spelling of his name pretentious and drops one 'a.']

The discussion of Cain and Abel touches on issues of guilt, arbitrary judgments and free will which are central to the novel. God's preference for Abel has already been repeated in Cyrus's seemingly arbitrary favoring of Adam over Charles. Strangely, Adam fails to make the connection. Later, Adam will favor one of his boys over the other just as did his father.

Questions

25. Samuel tells Adam, "'I don't very much believe in blood ... I think when a man finds good or bad in his children he is seeing only what he planted there after they cleared the womb.'" What does Adam see when he looks at the twins which makes him think otherwise?

Chapter 23.

[1] Samuel's favorite daughter, Una, marries a photographer and moves to Oregon where she lives a harsh life and dies (perhaps by suicide) very young. Her death breaks Samuel who suddenly becomes an old man. Tom is unable to settle to any profession, though the narrator and his sister idealize him. Dessie runs a successful dress shop in Salinas, but she falls in love with man who cannot, or will not, marry her and the joy goes out of her life. Tom comes to town looking for revenge against the man, but the sheriff has been tipped off by Samuel.

[2] At Thanksgiving 1911, the family gathers at the Hamilton ranch. Realizing how old their father has become they secretly come up with the

idea of their parents leaving the ranch and visiting each of them in turn.

[3] When he gets the letter with the first invitation, Samuel knows exactly what has been planned and why, but he agrees and so (more surprisingly) does Liza. This chapter shows the Hamiltons as a loving, mutually supportive family unit.

Questions

26. Why does Steinbeck at this point in the narrative give portraits of the lives of Una, Dessie and Tom? (Clue: What do their lives have in common?)

27. What does Samuel mean when, right at the end of the chapter, he tells Tom, "'I know where I am going, and I am content'"?

Chapter 24.

[1] Samuel pays a final visit to Adam. The twins are now eleven; Samuel notices that Adam loves Aron more than he loves Cal. The ranch has remained unplanted, but Samuel goads Adam into wanting to start planting the garden he once planned, but refuses to stay and do the work for him.

[2] Over dinner, Samuel learns that Cal looks forward to tending an acre that Adam will give him while Aron already raises hares, one of which he intends to give his father next birthday. (Cain was a farmer and Abel a herdsman.) Lee is obviously uncomfortable by how closely the brothers mirror the Cain and Abel myth. This story is discussed by the men after dinner. Lee declares that the original Hebrew word is *timshel* meaning "thou mayest." Thus, Cain was *not* fated to kill his brother; God granted him the freedom to overcome sin. Lee finds this a liberating idea.

[3] Before he leaves, Samuel tells Adam that Cathy (now Kate) runs a depraved brothel in Salinas. He hopes that knowing this will finally cure Adam of his love for Cathy. When asked by Lee, Samuel says that it was what Lee had said about *timshel* that had given him a motive to tell Adam the truth.

Notes:

Chautauqua was an adult education movement, founded in New York State in 1874, that was highly popular in the late nineteenth and early twentieth centuries. It brought together entertainment, speakers and preachers.

Questions

28. Is the anti-deterministic theory of morality opened up by Lee's

East of Eden by John Steinbeck

definition of *timshel* applicable to Cathy? Why? Why not?

Chapter 25.

[1] Next spring at the Hamilton ranch, Tom receives a telegram informing him of Samuel's death.

[2] Adam attends Samuel's funeral in Salinas.

[3] Adam goes to the whorehouse that Cathy runs and gets to see her. Cathy is still pretty, but age is subtly taking its toll on her body. She shows him compromising photographs of prominent men which she intends to use for blackmail and ultimately to destroy them. Her attempts to seduce Adam fail; he tells her that he is finally seeing her as she is not as he had dreamed that she was. Cathy senses her loss of power: she tells him that Charles is the real father of his twins and has Adam beaten by her bouncer.

Questions

29. Cathy explains her immorality by her belief that there is nothing in the world but evil and folly. She says that from her earliest childhood she knew that every appearance of goodness was merely a cloak to hide depravity. Contrast this view of human nature with Lee's definition of *timshel*.

Chapter 26.

[1] Adam feels finally free of Cathy. Before returning to his ranch, he stops in at Will Hamilton's garage and orders a car.

[2] When he gets home, Adam talks to Lee about his new feeling. Lee in turn shares his wish to run a book shop in San Francisco.

Chapter 27.

[1] Cal and Aron are out hunting rabbits. The two boys love each other deeply but there are tensions between them. In a moment of bitterness, Cal tells Aron that he heard some men saying that their mother had run away; Aron repeats his father's explanation that she is in heaven, but the idea of her running away disturbs him.

[2] The boys return home to find Mr. and Mrs. Bacon and their daughter Abra at the house having taken shelter from the rainstorm. The three children are sent out to play.

[3] Mr. Bacon talks about the need to educate the twins. He suggests that Adam should rent his ranch and move to the city where he could send his sons to public school. Suddenly, Adam wants very much to see his brother Charles again.

[4] Cal almost instantly falls in love with Abra and sensing that Abra (like just about everyone else) prefers Aron to him, when Aron leaves to get a present for her, Cal sets out to mock and scare her to get his revenge.

Aron and Cal are very similar to the young Adam and Charles: Aron has a light complexion and is friendly, honest, and trusting; Cal has a dark complexion and is jealous, manipulative, and troubled. Cal's determination to one day find his mother (though he has no idea where she is) and bring her back foreshadows looming disaster.

Questions

30. Comment on the symbolism of the storm which overtakes the twins when they are outside, "Aron turned around to look at the black monster…"

31. Explain how Cal sets out to belittle and discomfort Abra as soon as Aron leaves. Exactly why does Abra throw away the box that Aron has given her? Why is Aron so heart-broken about it?

Chapter 28.

[1] That evening, the twins find their father, for the first time, to be genuinely interested in them. Aron reveals that he wants to marry Abra, but Cal disturbs the pleasant atmosphere by asking where their mother is buried. Adam tells him that her body had been shipped back East for burial.

[2] Lee urges Adam to tell the boys the truth about their mother and warns of the consequences if they should find out about her and discover that their father had lied to them. He then tells Adam the terrible story of his own mother's death (she was the victim of multiple rape) to illustrate the importance of acknowledging the truth however terrible it is.

[3] Adam writes to his brother Charles for the first time in a decade inviting him to come to California for a visit

Questions

32. How does the story of Lee's parents fit into the wider themes of the novel?

Chapter 29.

[1-2] Will Hamilton delivers the new Ford but cannot explain how to start it. The following day a mechanic comes to explain how the car works. This chapter offers a little comic relief since no one (including the mechanic) actually understands the workings of the internal combustion engine.

East of Eden by John Steinbeck

Chapter 30

[1] A week later, Adam drives Lee and the twins into town. He picks up a letter from solicitors informing him of the death of Charles who has left his money ($100,000) equally to Adam and to Cathy. Cal tells Aron that his father will send them to bed early to talk to Lee and that he intends to listen to what they say. Aron asks his brother why he does, "'All the tricky, sneaky things.'" Cal has no answer for his brother; he feels bad about his meanness and longs for Aron to love him.

[2] Adam discusses with Lee the moral dilemma posed by Charles' will. Lee senses that Adam has already decided that he must give Cathy her share.

[3] Having secretly listened, Cal now knows that his mother is still alive. Aware that this knowledge is a powerful weapon he prays fervently not to be mean and manipulative but to be like Aron. He lies to Aron telling him that their father discussed plans to send a wreath to their mother's grave.

Questions

33. In what way is Cal presented in a more sympathetic light toward the end of this chapter?

Chapter 31.

[1] Adam travels to Salinas where he tells Cathy about the $50,000 she inherits from Charles' will. Cathy cannot believe that Adam is simply doing what he considers to be the right thing; Adam tells Cathy that she does not understand that good and evil coexist in most people - she sees only the evil.

[2] Adam calls in on Liza who is living with Olive's family. Liza asks him to go to see Tom because she is concerned about him. His sister Dessie is considering giving up her dressmaking business and moving back to the ranch to be with Tom.

Questions

34. Adam says that Cathy sees only the evil in men. How does this judgment relate to the story Lee tells about his mother's death? (Clue: Look particularly at how Lee concludes his tale.)

Chapter 32.

[1] Dessie's business has declined since her disappointment in love made her sad. Will tries to persuade her not to live at the ranch with Tom because he thinks Tom is unstable since their father's death.

[2] Dessie is met at the train station by Tom and taken back to the ranch.

A Study Guide

Adam has bought her Salinas house. Both Tom and Dessie are happy about the move. However, Dessie suffers from pains in her side which foreshadow "sadness and death."

Notes:

Chatterbox was a popular periodical for children in the nineteenth century produced by Frank Leslie (1821 - 80).

Chapter 33.

[1] Dessie and Tom plan to work for a year to get enough money to visit Europe. Tom goes into town to ask Will for a loan to buy one hundred young pigs.

[2] When he returns, he finds Dessie in great pain and gives her a laxative. When she gets worse, he goes to a neighbor to phone the doctor.

[3] A week after Dessie's funeral, Tom comes back to the ranch. He sends a letter to Will telling him to explain his death to their mother as a riding accident, and then he shoots himself.

Questions

35. Tom is the fourth character to commit suicide, the first being Cyrus' unnamed first wife. Who are the others? What error does each of these characters make in deciding to commit suicide? How does Lee's understanding of *timshel* help the reader to see that these characters are wrong to kill themselves?

36. Three of Samuel's children are now dead. What aspects of character did they have in common? How did they differ from the siblings who survive (of whom Will is typical)?

Chapter 34.

The narrator ruminates on the story of man and its meaning concluding that it is about "the never-ending contest in ourselves of good and evil." Each generation faces the same struggle against evil - that is the essence of the human condition.

Notes:

Pearl White (1889 - 1938) was a stage and film actress who, from 1914-20, starred in a number of serials for the cinema including *The Perils of Pauline.*

The three men referred to (but unnamed) are respectively: J. D. Rockefeller (1839-1937), director of Standard Oil; William Randolph Hearst (1863-1951), the newspaper owner; and F. D. Roosevelt (1882-

East of Eden by John Steinbeck

1945), who was president during the Great Depression of the 1930s.

Chapter 35.

[1-2] Having supervised the move to Salinas, Lee leaves for San Francisco to open his bookshop. Six days after he leaves he comes back telling Adam, "'I've never been so goddam lonesome in my life.'"

Chapter 36.

[1] Aron and Cal settle into their high school where both are good students. Aron is popular; Cal is respected for his skills.

[2] Aron and Abra develop an understanding that they will eventually get married. Promising him to secrecy, Abra tells Aron that she overheard her parents say that Adam's wife is still alive.

[3] This idea confuses Aron: he has always wanted a mother and hopes Abra's secret is true, but if it is then his father and Lee would be liars and he would lose his faith in them. For the moment that faith holds.

Notes:

The pre-Raphaelites were a group of artists in mid-nineteenth century England dedicated to a revival of medieval culture - literally to take painting back to the period before Raphael the Italian Renaissance painter and architect.

Chapter 37.

[1] In 1915, Lee buys an ice box (*not* a refrigerator) for the house. Adam becomes fascinated by it and experiments with preserving food by icing. He talks to Will about buying the town's ice plant and using ice to ship fresh vegetables to the North-east in winter. Will appears skeptical, though privately he is interested in the plan.

[2] Adam puts his scheme into practice, but the train carrying his iced lettuce to New York is delayed, and the lettuce is spoiled when it arrives. Adam loses a lot of money and becomes a target for mockery in the town where stories about his past begin to circulate.

[3] Noticing the reaction of people to his father's failed scheme, Aron tells Abra that it will make a big difference to their future, but she tells him she is determined to marry him no matter what. Aron blames his father for the failure of the lettuce scheme and tells Abra that he thinks his father lied about their mother. She releases him from his promise and tells him to just ask Adam. Aron is evasive and rushes away.

Chapter 38.

The narrative has reached the point where Cal and Aron have become the main characters. The reader becomes increasingly sympathetic to Cal as the narrator explains his moral struggles.

[1] Even in Salinas, Cal remains without friends yet desperately needing love, particularly from his father.

[2] Cal takes to walking alone late at night. Once he encounters a farmer from the valley who is drunk. The man takes Cal to Kate's; Cal is revolted by the depravity he witnesses there.

[3] One night, Cal tells Lee that he knows the truth about his mother. Lee honestly answers his questions. When Cal says that he feels his mother in himself, Lee angrily tells him that he also has his father's goodness - like all men, he is a mixture of good and evil.

[4] "[In] Cal there grew a passionate love for his father and a wish to protect him and make it up to him for the things he had suffered." Aron becomes very religious, tries to convert Cal and tells Abra that he wants to stay celibate all his life. Like Cyrus' first wife and Tom Hamilton, Aron triumphs over "sins he had never committed."

Questions

37. What differences do you notice in the way in which Aron and Cal react to the failure of their father's lettuce scheme?

38. Since it is now clearly foreshadowed that Aron will eventually discover the truth about his mother, speculate on how you think that might happen and how you think that he will react.

Chapter 39

[1] In the autumn of 1916 Cal is picked up in a raid on a Chinese gambling house, and Adam has to collect him from jail. Cal expects to be punished, but instead Adam opens up to him about his own arrest. Cal admits that he knows about his mother but says that Aron could not stand knowing about her. Adam tells Cal that he trusts him. For the first time, Cal is truly happy.

[2] With greater self-confidence, Cal takes to following Cathy when she goes out on Monday afternoons. One time she confronts him, and he tells her who he is. Cal tells his mother that he is no longer afraid that he has her evil in him and that he is his own person. It is Cathy who is afraid of Cal because she knows she is powerless to manipulate him, as she had been with Samuel.

East of Eden by John Steinbeck

Notes:

Fan-tan is a traditional Chinese betting game. A double handful of counters is placed on the table and covered up. Gamblers now bet on 1, 2, 3 or 4. The counters are uncovered and counted off in groups of four until four or fewer remain. If 4 remain, then those who bet on 4 win; if 3, then those who bet on 3 win; and so on.

Chapter 40

[1-2] Some time before this Ethel, a former whore in Faye's house, came to Cathy and attempted to blackmail her by suggesting that she had evidence that Cathy had murdered Faye. Cathy had her run out of town on trumped up charges. The incident with Ethel generated the same fear she felt after talking to Cal.

[3] Following this incident with Ethel, Cathy becomes more reclusive, always fearful that the truth might come out. She senses Charles Trask's presence. (Remember when Charles wrote to his brother that he sensed the farmhouse was haunted?).

Chapter 41.

[1] Involvement in the war in Europe comes inevitably closer.

[2] Cal convinces Aron to try to graduate high school a year early so that he can go to college. This will minimize the danger of him finding out the truth about his mother. Cal promises to help him through college.

[3] Cal goes to talk to Will Hamilton about how to make $20-30,000 so that he can give Adam the amount he lost on the lettuce scheme. It is agreed that, with the $5,000 he can borrow from Lee, they will become partners in buying beans. They can contract to buy beans from local farmers at a low price knowing they will be able to sell them to English agents for a substantial profit.

Questions

39. Why does Cal want to give his father money? (His motivation is complex!)

Chapter 42.

Only gradually does the reality of the war begin to impact the people of Salinas.

Notes:

General Pershing (1860 - 1948) would lead the U. S. Expeditionary Forces to victory in the First World War in November 1918. On March 15, 1916, he led an unsuccessful expedition into Mexico to capture the revolutionary

Pancho Villa (1878-1923).

Chapter 43.
[1] Lee tells Adam that Aron is studying through the summer in order to graduate a year early. Adam is very proud and immediately plans a party and the gift of an engraved gold watch.

[2] Rev. Rolf, who is helping Aron with his studying, describes a woman who has come to services for the last five weeks. He has discovered that she runs a brothel in the town. He does not know that this is Cathy or that she is there to spy on Aron.

[3] Liza Hamilton dies. On the day he gets his exam results, Aron says nothing to his father about having passed and goes out to dinner with Rev. Rolf. Cal feels like beating him up, but Lee restrains him. Later Lee counsels Aron to tell his father about his examination success because it means a lot to Adam. Aron says that he did not think his father cared and that all he wants to do is to get away from Salinas.

Chapter 44.
[1] With Aron away at Stanford, Abra spends more time at the Trask house, particularly with Lee. She tells him that she worries that Aron has idealized his absent mother and projected that idealization onto her. Abra knows that she is not as perfect as Aron conceives her. Abra describes Aron's resentment against his father for his business failure. She asks Lee if Aron's mother is still alive, and he confirms it. In Abra's presence, Cal tells Lee that he has made enough money to pay back his $5,000, with $15,000 in interest. Cal plans to give the money to his father on Thanksgiving.

[2] Cal and Abra talk. He admits to visiting whorehouses, and she admits to being bad as well.

The SparkNotes writer makes this important distinction, "Aron chooses a life of security and illusion, while Cal struggles to be moral amid the realities and evils of the world." Ironically, Adam repeats the mistake of his own father by putting his faith in the apparent ambition of Aron and lamenting Cal's lack of drive.

Questions
40. Predict Adam's reaction when Cal presents him with the money he has made. (Explain your reasons in detail.)

Chapter 45.
[1] Joe Valery is Cathy's 'muscle' at the whorehouse. Although he is

frightened of Cathy, he is always looking for a way to get ahead.

[2] Regretting that she let Ethel out of her hands, Cathy offers Joe $500 if he can find her in one of the border towns. Before he leaves, she lets him know that she has evidence that he is an escaped convict.

[3] Joe travels out of town and enquires after Ethel, eventually discovering that she is dead. Joe thinks deeply about how to turn what he knows to his advantage.

[4] Cathy wakes feeling much better; her new medicine has taken the way the pain of the arthritis in her hands. Joe reports that he could not find Ethel but heard a rumor that she planned to come back to Salinas and lie low. Although Cathy attempts to appear nonchalant, Joe sees the fear in her reaction and knows he has a weapon against her.

Questions

41. In the battle between Joe and Cathy who will be the winner? Justify your answer.

Chapter 46.

The narrator recalls with sadness the anti-German sentiment in Salinas and how he and his sister tormented a local tailor, Mr. Fenchel, because of his German accent. Others set Fenchel's house on fire. There were also acts of heroism. And some businessmen made a lot of money from the war through speculation.

Chapter 47.

[1] Adam is appointed to the draft board. He agonizes over decisions about which men should be enlisted and which excused on medical grounds.

[2] Adam discusses his moral dilemma with Lee who reminds him of the meaning of *timshel*.

[3] Aron is unhappy at Stamford because it does not live up to his exalted, pure vision of it. He is thinking of leaving.

Questions

42. How do you think that Adam's experience on the draft board will influence the way he reacts to Cal's gift of money?

Chapter 48.

[1-2] The Nigger, madam of one of the three whorehouses in Salinas, dies. All the old-timers are passing on. Joe meets Alf, the town handyman, and gets him to talk about Faye's death.

[3] Joe hints to Cathy that Ethel has been seen in Salinas and she tells him

to find her.

[4] Cathy questions one of her girls about the details of the Nigger's funeral.

Questions

43. Cathy appears different in this chapter. How and why is she changing?

44. What is the significance of the capsule of morphine that she wears around her neck?

Chapter 49.

This chapter presents the climax of the novel, the dramatic incidents up to which the entire narrative has been leading.

[1] Aron arrives home from college. He hints to Abra that he is unhappy there.

[2] Aron feels trapped by his father's ambitions for him (ironically just as Adam had felt about his father sending him into the cavalry) and tells Cal of his desire to leave college. Cal hints that after college they could go into partnership. Cal gives Aron the money to buy champagne for Thanksgiving dinner.

[3] Just after Thanksgiving dinner, Cal gives his father the money he has made, but Adam rejects it telling him that he could not benefit from war profiteering. Cal bolts to his room and feels "hate … seeping through all of his body."

[4] Cal pretends to Lee and his father that he is not upset by what has happened. He goes out looking for Aron who has walked Abra home. Cal tells his brother he has something interesting to show him.

[5] A young man, claiming to be 18 years old, presents himself at the San Jose recruiting office next morning.

Notes:

Adam's rejection of Cal's money parallels God's rejection of Cain's offering by giving preference to the offering from Abel. This action prompts Cain to kill Abel out of jealousy. Adam's rejection of Cal's gift also parallels Cyrus's rejection of Charles's gift. In all three cases, a father arbitrarily gives his love to one son over another.

Questions

45. It takes no great effort to realize that the young man is Aron. Fill in the gap in the narrative between parts 4 and 5. Why does Aron want to join the Army? (His reasons are many and complex. The reader probably understands them much better than does the character.)

East of Eden by John Steinbeck

46. Why is Aron totally unable to cope with the reality of who and what Cathy is? (Remember that for many years Adam could not bring himself to accept the same reality.)

Chapter 50

[1] Cathy has been awake all night since the visit of Cal and Aron; the pain in her hands is excruciating. She has seen and understood the look of cruelty in Cal's eyes, but the goodness she has seen in Aron's face has been alien to her. Joe enters and suggests that Ethel has asked to see him. Cathy becomes suspicious and traps him so that she knows he is working against her. When he leaves, she writes a will in which she leaves all her worldly possessions to Aron and then a note to the sheriff telling him to check on Joe's fingerprints. Alone in her room she takes the morphine capsule.

[2] In the morning, Joe discovers her body, but almost immediately he is picked up by a deputy and is shot dead trying to escape.

Notes:
The Winning of Barbara Worth was a 1911 bestselling historical novel by Harold Bell Wright (1872-1944) set in the barren lands of San Diego County.

Questions

47. Comment on the symbolic significance of Cathy leaving all of her money to Aron. (Clue: Remember that Cyrus left his questionable fortune to Adam and Charles, and that Charles passed on his portion, untouched, to Adam on his death.)

Chapter 51.

[1] Sheriff Quinn checks on the legality of Cathy's will. He destroys the incriminating photographs of prominent men in the town which Cathy intended to use to destroy them. Then Quinn goes to tell Adam about Cathy's legacy to Aron. Aron, however, has not been home for two days; when he is asked, Cal denies any knowledge of where he is.

[2] Lee finds Cal burning the money he made for his father; he tells him that all humans are a mix of good and evil; he is not unique and his fate is not tragic; but it is in their power to choose between them. Adam returns home with a short letter from Aron saying that he has joined the Army. Adam feels faint and unwell.

A Study Guide

Notes:

Genesis 4.9: "And the LORD said unto Cain, Where *is* Abel thy brother? And he said, I know not: *Am* I my brother's keeper?" (KJV).

Questions

48. Comment on Adam's physical reaction when Cal denies knowledge of and responsibility for his brother.

49. Explain the relevance to the <u>themes</u> of the narrative of the section from *The Meditations of Marcus Aurelius* that Lee reads.

Chapter 52.

[1] In the winter of 1917-18, it seems to the people of Salinas that the war will be lost.

[2] Adam struggles to understand why Aron joined the Army; he also struggles with his balance, circulation and eyesight. Lee tells Cal to ask Abra to come round.

[3] Cal meets Abra and tells her the truth about what he did to cause Aron to run away. Abra informs Cal that Aron has ended their relationship. She says that Aron built a fantasy relationship that could never survive reality, and she tells Cal that she loves him because he is not good like his brother.

[4] Abra returns home. Her father is feeling ill and has not been out, but she has a feeling he is actually hiding. Judge Knudson had been trying to get in touch with him but has been told that Mr. Bacon cannot see anyone.

Questions

50. How would you explain the 'illness' of Abra's father?

Chapter 53.

[1-3] Abra visits the Trask house. Adam, feeling a little better, is out, and Cal is not yet home from drill. Lee tells her that he wishes that she were his daughter.

[4] Cal walks Abra home. Cal wonders where his mother is buried and contemplates putting flowers on her grave. It occurs to him that he is thinking like Aron.

Questions

51. Contrast the 'parenting' of Abra by Lee and by her real mother.

52. Comment on the <u>symbolism</u> of the collar of Cal's uniform which is irritating his neck.

Chapter 54.

[1-4] In May, 1918, the American forces win their first significant victory over the Germans. Cal has promised to take Abra on a picnic when the

East of Eden by John Steinbeck

azaleas come out, but winter is long, and it is not until the end of May that Cal and Abra skip school to gather the azaleas. Abra shares with Cal her suspicion that her father has embezzled money from his firm and is afraid of being prosecuted - this proves, she says, that Cal is not the only person who does wrong.

[5] Lee receives a telegram reporting Aron's death. He sees Aron as having taken a coward's way out by abandoning the real world. Lee has to break the news to Adam when he gets home.

Chapter 55.

[1] Cal returns home to find his father in bed. He has suffered a stroke, and Dr. Edwards and Dr. Murphy are examining him. Adam is largely paralyzed, but the prognosis is uncertain. When Cal sees Adam, he tells him of his guilt over Aron's death and thinks he sees anger in his eyes. A nurse arrives. Lee advises Cal to go to Abra.

[2] Cal goes to the Bacon house, and Abra skips out the back to join him. She insists that he returns home with her and faces his father.

[3] Lee asks Adam to forgive Cal, and Adam whispers the word *timshel*.

The resolution of the novel is that Cal finally receives his father's blessing; Cal now knows that he can choose the path of goodness, that he will never be perfectly good, but that he does not have to feel guilty about this. Cal also has the love of Abra - a real, human love which will survive the realities of the world. Children are not automatically doomed to repeat their parents' mistakes. Without Lee's care and love, none of this would have been possible.

Notes:

Marguerite of Navarre (1492-1549), sister of King Francis I, wrote the *Hetameron* a collection of seventy-two short stories which was published posthumously in 1558. Many deal with love, lust, infidelity, and sexual relationships.

Questions

53. Steinbeck is frequently criticized for being sentimental. How effective do you find the resolution of the novel?

A Study Guide

Further Reading: A personal note

I first read *East of Eden* when I was sixteen. The novel drew me entirely into its world, and I felt that I knew the characters that became 'real' in a way that I had not previously experienced. It was not until I got to university that my teachers assured me that Steinbeck was not a 'great' writer, scarcely a 'good' writer. I will leave you to make up your own mind on that.

Steinbeck wrote in his journal before each day's stint of writing on the novel. These 'letters' were published as *Journal of a Novel* and are certainly worth reading in conjunction with *East of Eden*.

If you want to read another John Steinbeck novel, let it be *In Dubious Battle*. Largely forgotten now, it is in my opinion his greatest work.

Perspectives

Discuss the following opinions:

1. "[Writers are] delegated to declare and to celebrate man's proven capacity for greatness of heart and spirit ... [a] writer who does not passionately believe in the perfectibility of man, has no dedication nor any membership in literature" (Steinbeck Nobel Lecture). To what extent does *East of Eden* embody these values?

2. "We see in novel after novel belief in science, a firm belief in material causation, a belief in the spontaneous goodness of simple men, and a radical distrust of commerce, industry, and the business outlook, and conventional piety and morality" (Walcutt "John Steinbeck's Naturalism" 1954). To what extent does that generalization apply to *East of Eden*?

Assignments

1. Explain how Cyrus infects his entire family with evil following his return from the Civil War.
2. In what ways do Charles and Adam play out the story of Cain and Abel?
3. Contrast the marital roles of Cyrus' two wives with that of Liza Hamilton.
4. What are Samuel Hamilton's personal qualities? What are his limitations?
5. How does Lee transcend the limitations of being Chinese in turn-of-the-century America?

East of Eden by John Steinbeck

6. In what ways do Cal and Aron play out the story of Cain and Abel?

7. What is the role of Abra in Cal's redemption?

8. Examine one of the stories involving members of the Hamilton family (e.g., Will's success in business or Dessie and Tom setting up home at the ranch). How does this minor plot relate to the major themes of the novel?

9. The children of Samuel and Liza have widely different lives. What factors account for the life that each leads? Do you find any pattern in the lives of the nine children?

Works Cited:

SparkNotes Editors. "SparkNote on *East of Eden*." SparkNotes.com. SparkNotes LLC. 2003. Web. 11 May 2015.

TheBestNotes.com Staff. "TheBestNotes on *East of Eden*". TheBestNotes.com. 19 August 2014. Web. 26 May 2015.

A Study Guide

Literary Terms

As you use each term in the study guide, fill in the definition of the term and include an example from the text to show how it is used. The first definition is supplied. Find an example in the text to complete it.

Term	Definition
	Example
climax	*The climax of a plot occurs when the suspense (between protagonist and antagonist) reaches its peak*
foreshadow	
irony (ironically)	
metaphor	
narrator	

East of Eden by John Steinbeck

Term	Definition
	Example
omniscient/limited	
protagonist	
resolution	
setting	
symbolism (symbolic, symbolically)	

A Study Guide

Term	Definition
	Example
theme	

East of Eden by John Steinbeck

Selected Literary Terms - Definitions

NOTE: Not all of these terms may be relevant to this particular study guide

Allegorical: a story in which the characters, their actions and the settings represent abstract ideas (often moral ideas) or historical/political events.

Ambiguous, ambiguity: when a statement is unclear in meaning – ambiguity may be deliberate or accidental.

Analogy: a comparison which treats two things as identical in one or more specified ways.

Antagonist: a character or force opposing the protagonist.

Antithesis: the complete opposite of something.

Authorial comment: when the writer addresses the reader directly (not to be confused with the narrator doing so).

Climax: the conflict to which the action has been building since the start of the play or story.

Colloquialism: the casual, informal mainly spoken language of ordinary people – often called "slang."

Comic hyperbole: deliberately inflated, extravagant language used for comic effect.

Comic Inversion: reversing the normally accepted order of things for comic effect.

Connotation: the ideas, feelings and associations generated by a word or phrase.

Dark comedy: comedy which has a serious implication – comedy that deals with subjects not usually treated humorously (e.g., death).

Deus ex machina: an unnatural or very unlikely turn of events in a story that resolves or removes one or more problems faced by a character or characters.

Dialogue: a conversation between two or more people in direct speech.

Diction: the writer's choice of words in order to create a particular effect.

Equivocation: saying something which is capable of two interpretations with the intention of misrepresenting the truth.

Euphemism: a polite word for an ugly truth – for example, a person is said to be sleeping when they are actually dead.

A Study Guide

Fallacy: a misconception resulting from incorrect reasoning.

First person: first person singular is "I" and plural is "we".

Foreshadow: a statement or action which gives the reader a hint of what is likely to happen later in the narrative.

Form of speech: the register in which speech is written – the diction reflects the character.

Frame narrative: a story within which the main narrative is placed.

Genre: the type of literature into which a particular text falls (e.g. drama, poetry, novel).

Hubris: pride – in Greek tragedy it is the hero's belief that he can challenge the will of the gods.

Hyperbole: exaggeration designed to create a particular effect.

Image, imagery: figurative language such as simile, metaphor, personification etc., or a description which conjures up a particularly vivid picture.

Imply, implication: when the text suggests to the reader a meaning which it does not actually state.

Infer, inference: the reader's act of going beyond what is stated in the text to draw conclusions.

Irony, ironic: a form of humor which undercuts the apparent meaning of a statement:

> *Conscious irony:* irony used deliberately by a writer or character;
>
> *Unconscious irony:* a statement or action which has significance for the reader of which the character is unaware;
>
> *Dramatic irony*: when an action has an important significance that is obvious to the reader but not to one or more of the characters;
>
> *Tragic irony:* when a character says (or does) something which will have a serious, even fatal, consequence for him/ her. The audience is aware of the error, but the character is not;
>
> *Verbal irony*: the conscious use of particular words which are appropriate to what is being said.

Juxtaposition: literally putting two things side by side for purposes of comparison and/ or contrast.

Literal: the surface level of meaning that a statement has.

East of Eden by John Steinbeck

Melodramatic: action and/or dialogue that is inflated or extravagant – frequently used for comic effect.

Metaphor, metaphorical: the description of one thing by direct comparison with another (e.g. the coal-black night).

   Extended metaphor: a comparison which is developed at length.

Microcosm: literally 'the world is little' – a situation which reflects truths about the world in general.

Mood: the feelings and emotions contained in and/ or produced by a work of art (text, painting, music, etc.).

Motif: a frequently repeated idea, image or situation in a text.

Motivation: why a character acts as he/she does – in modern literature motivation is seen as psychological.

Narrator: the voice that the reader hears in the text – not to be confused with the author.

Frame narrative /story: a story within which the main story is told (e.g. *Heart of Darkness* by Conrad begins with five men on a boat in the Thames and then one of them tells the story of his experiences on the river Congo).

Oxymoron: the juxtaposition of two terms normally thought of as opposite (e.g. the silent scream).

Parable: a story with a moral lesson (e.g. the Good Samaritan).

Paradox, paradoxical: a statement or situation which appears self-contradictory and therefore absurd.

Pathos: is pity, or rather the ability of a text to make the audience or reader feel pity.

Perspective: point of view from which a story, or an incident within a story, is told.

Personified, personification: a simile or metaphor in which an inanimate object or abstract idea is described by comparison with a human.

Plot: a chain of events linked by cause and effect.

Prologue: an introduction which gives a lead-in to the main story.

Protagonist: the character who initiates the action and is most likely to have the sympathy of the audience.

Pun: a deliberate play on words where a particular word has two or more meanings both appropriate in some way to what is being said.

Realism: a text that describes the action in a way that appears to reflect life.

Rhetoric: any use of language designed to make the expression of ideas more effective (e.g. repetition, imagery, alliteration, etc.).

Sarcasm: stronger than irony – it involves a deliberate attack on a person or idea with the intention of mocking.

Satire, Satiric: the use of comedy to criticize attack, belittle, or humiliate – more extreme than irony.

Setting: the environment in which the narrative (or part of the narrative) takes place.

Simile: a description of one thing by explicit comparison with another (e.g. my love is like a red, red rose).

Extended simile: a comparison which is developed at length.

Style: the way in which a writer chooses to express him/ herself. Style is a vital aspect of meaning since how something is expressed can crucially affect what is being written or spoken.

Suspense: the building of tension in the reader.

Symbol, symbolic, symbolism, symbolize: a physical object which comes to represent an abstract idea (e.g. the sun may symbolize life).

Themes: important concepts, beliefs and ideas explored and presented in a text.

Third person: third person singular is "he/ she/ it" and plural is "they" – authors often write novels in the third person.

Tone: literally the sound of a text – How words sound (either in the mouth of an actor or the head of a reader) can crucially affect meaning/

Tragic: King Richard III and Macbeth are both murderous tyrants, yet only Macbeth is a *tragic* figure. Why? Because Macbeth has the potential to be great, recognizes the error he has made and all that he has lost in making it, and dies bravely in a way that seems to accept the justice of the punishment.

East of Eden by John Steinbeck

Classroom Use of the Study Guide Questions

The aim of a Study Guide is to *support not to replace* the reading of the text. That is why there are no answers to the study questions. Every reader has to find the answers in the text. Trust the students to do this. They may come up with things you have never thought of.

Although there are both closed and open questions in the Study Guide, very few of them have simple, right or wrong answers. They are designed to encourage in-depth discussion, disagreement, and (eventually) consensus. Above all, they aim to encourage students to go to the text to support their conclusions and interpretations.

I am not so arrogant as to presume to tell teachers how they should use this resource. I used it in the following ways, each of which ensured that students were well prepared for class discussion and presentations.

1. Set a reading assignment for the class and tell everyone to be aware that the questions will be the focus of whole class discussion the next class.

2. Set a reading assignment for the class and allocate particular questions to sections of the class (e.g. if there are four questions, divide the class into four sections, etc.). In class, form discussion groups containing one person who has prepared each question and allow time for feedback within the groups. Have feedback to the whole class on each question by picking a group at random to present their answers and to follow up with class discussion.

3. Set a reading assignment for the class, but do not allocate questions. In class, divide students into groups and allocate to each group one of the questions related to the reading assignment the answer to which they will have to present formally to the class. Allow time for discussion and preparation.

4. Set a reading assignment for the class, but do not allocate questions. In class, divide students into groups and allocate to each group one of the questions related to the reading assignment. Allow time for discussion and preparation. Now reconfigure the groups so that each group contains at least one person who has prepared each question and allow time for feedback within the groups.

5. Before starting to read the text, allocate specific questions to individuals or pairs. (It is best not to allocate all questions to allow for other approaches and variety. One in three questions or one in four seems about right.) Tell students that they will be leading the class discussion on their question. They will need to start with a brief presentation of the issues and then conduct a question and answer session. After this, they will be expected to present a brief review of the discussion.

6. Having finished the text, arrange the class into groups of 3, 4 or 5. Tell each group to select as many questions from the Study Guide as there are members of the group. Each individual is responsible for drafting out a written answer to one question, and each answer should be a substantial paragraph. Each group as a whole is then responsible for discussing, editing and suggesting improvements to each answer, which is revised by the original writer and brought back to the group for a final proof reading followed by revision. This seems to work best when the group knows that at least some of the points for the activity will be based on the quality of all of the answers.

East of Eden by John Steinbeck

Graphic Organizers

Plot graph for *East of Eden*: The Conflict between Adam and Charles

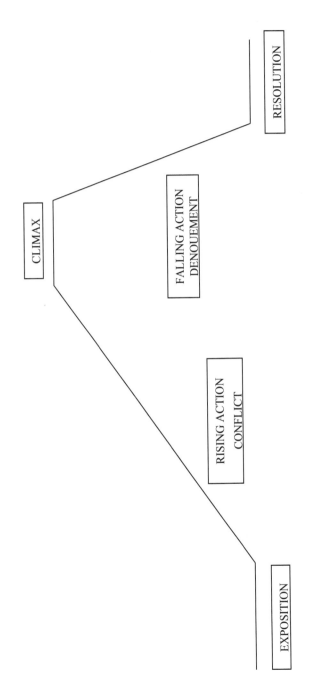

EXPOSITION

RISING ACTION
CONFLICT

CLIMAX

FALLING ACTION
DENOUEMENT

RESOLUTION

A Study Guide

Plot graph for *East of Eden*: The Conflict between Adam and Caleb

CLIMAX

RESOLUTION

FALLING ACTION
DENOUEMENT

RISING ACTION
CONFLICT

EXPOSITION

To the Reader

The Reverend Lyle Thorne Mysteries

If you enjoy detective short stories, you will love my series featuring policeman turned vicar Lyle Thorne (1860-1947)

Investigations of The Reverend Lyle Thorne (Volume One)

Thorne investigates five cases spanning the years 1911-1927:

- The fallen woman loses more than her life...
- The anonymous cleric pleads for a murder suspect...
- The Italian bride is frightened by mysterious disappearances...
- The missing betrothed vanishes the day before her wedding...
- A hanged man is still swinging in a locked room...

Further Investigations of The Reverend Lyle Thorne (Volume Two)

Thorne investigates five cases spanning the years 1910-1912:

- The wedding of an American heiress and divorcee is cancelled by the inexplicable disappearance of her ring...
- An Oxford antiquarian is found lying on a hoard of medieval coins...
- The young bride-to-be of a rich widower receives frightening threats...
- A Sussex landowner walks calmly into the courtyard of his house and vanishes...
- Thorne must find a husband who has taken great care not to be found...

Early Investigations of Lyle Thorne (Volume Three)

Thorne investigates five cases spanning the years 1876 to 1889:

- In Thorne's first ever investigation, his father is accused of murder by a dead man...
- Having been told to meet his step-father at 1 p.m., a young boy sets off from home at 12.45 p.m. and is never seen alive again...
- Twins plan and execute a perfect murder...
- A baby disappears from the nursery of the London home of the Duke and Duchess of Albermarle...
- Thorne's investigations put a name to Jack the Ripper but at terrible personal cost...

Sanditon Investigations of The Rev. Lyle Thorne (Volume Four)
Thorne investigates five cases spanning the years 1912-1914:

- A young girl disappears for the second time, this time from an enclosed garden...
- A modern painter dies of a heart attack – a natural death until the coffin falls and breaks open at the burial...
- A bishop in line to become Archbishop of Canterbury is poisoned in his own library...
- Thorne's curate encounters a young girl abandoned on the promenade...
- The discovery of the body of a man stabbed to death more than two centuries ago sets Thorne the ultimate investigative challenge...

Final Investigations of The Rev. Lyle Thorne (Volume Five)
Thorne investigates five cases spanning the years 1927-1948:

- A photographer's kiosk is burned down on the same day as Sanditon's biggest jewel robbery...
- A school master is found poisoned a few days before his retirement...
- A shell-shocked soldier becomes obsessed by "the lady in the dark"...
- A young railway worker implicated in a robbery is found murdered...
- Thorne witnesses the discovery of an 'impossible' murder-robbery at a bank in Sanditon...

Lost Investigation of The Rev. Lyle Thorne (Volume Six)
Thorne investigates five cases spanning the years 1908 - 1912:

- A runner is seen entering the tunnel under a railway line and is never seen again...
- Rev. Thorne's curate is accused of the theft of a valuable sapphire pendant from a dying woman...
- The body of a local man is washed up on Sanditon beach, but his empty cottage is found to be locked from the inside...
- The abrupt dismissal of a scullery maid alerts Thorne to two crimes...

- A mysterious and glamorous American widow is abducted, and the body of her abductor is found the next day…

Official Investigations of Lyle Thorne (Volume Seven)

As a young member of the Metropolitan Police, Thorne investigates five cases spanning the years 1881 – 1887:

- An apparently simple case of murder reveals Thorne's ability to see beyond the obvious…
- Three young women plan a holiday excursion to Margate, but events take a tragic turn…
- Thorne realizes that an innocent man will be hung and that it is his evidence that has convicted him…
- A weekly tea party leaves one woman dead and another in the hospital…
- An international criminal wagers the Commissioner of Police that he can commit the perfect crime…

Clerical Investigations of The Rev. Lyle Thorne (Volume Eight)

As a newly ordained minister in the Church of England, Thorne investigates three cases spanning the years 1896 – 1898:

- A curate inexplicably leaves his parish in the middle of the night, just as two years earlier the former vicar had also left…
- A vicar in Leeds is found kneeling over the dead body of his wife with the murder weapon in his hand…
- The manuscript of an ancient Lindisfarne gospel and its modern translation disappear from a locked strongbox, in a locked desk, in a locked room…

About the Author

Ray Moore was born in Nottingham, England. He obtained his Master's Degree in Literature from Lancaster University and taught in secondary education for twenty-eight years before relocating to Florida with his wife. There he taught English and Information Technology in the International Baccalaureate Program. He is now a full-time writer and fitness fanatic and leads a reading group at a local library.

Website: http://www.raymooreauthor.com

Ray strives to make his texts the best that they can be. If you have any comments or question about this book *please* contact the author through his email: **villageswriter@gmail.com**

Also by Ray Moore:

Books are available from amazon.com and from barnesandnoble.com as paperbacks and some from online eBook retailers.

Fiction:

The Lyle Thorne Mysteries Volumes One to Eight. (as detailed previously)

Non-fiction:

The *Critical Introduction series* is written for high school teachers and students and for college undergraduates. Each volume gives an in-depth analysis of a key text:

"The Stranger" by Albert Camus: A Critical Introduction (Revised Second Edition)

"The General Prologue" by Geoffrey Chaucer: A Critical Introduction

"Pride and Prejudice" by Jane Austen: A Critical Introduction

"The Great Gatsby" by F. Scott Fitzgerald: A Critical Introduction

The Text and Critical Introduction series differs from the Critical introduction series as these books contain the original text and in the case of the medieval texts an interlinear translation to aid the understanding of the text. The commentary allows the reader to develop a deeper understanding of the text and themes within the text.

*"Sir Gawain and the Green Knight": Text and Critical Introduction**

*"The General Prologue" by Geoffrey Chaucer: Text and Critical Introduction**

*"Heart of Darkness" by Joseph Conrad: Text and Critical Introduction**

*"Henry V" by William Shakespeare: Text and Critical Introduction**

"Oedipus Rex" by Sophocles: Text and Critical Introduction*
"A Room with a View" By E.M. Forster: Text and Critical Introduction*
"The Sign of Four" by Sir Arthur Conan Doyle Text and Critical Introduction
"The Wife of Bath's Prologue and Tale" by Geoffrey Chaucer: Text and Critical Introduction*
Jane Austen: The Complete Juvenilia: Text and Critical Introduction

Study guides - listed alphabetically by author

Study Guides offer an in-depth look at aspects of a text. They generally include an introduction to the characters, genre, themes, setting, tone of a text. They also may include activities on helpful literary terms as well as graphic organizers to aid understanding of the plot and different perspectives of characters.

* denotes also available as an eBook
"ME and EARL and the Dying GIRL" by Jesse Andrews: A Study Guide
Study Guide to "Alias Grace" by Margaret Atwood*
Study Guide to "The Handmaid's Tale" by Margaret Atwood*
"Pride and Prejudice" by Jane Austen: A Study Guide
"Moloka'i" by Alan Brennert: A Study Guide
"Wuthering Heights" by Emily Brontë: A Study Guide *
Study Guide on "Jane Eyre" by Charlotte Brontë*
"The Myth of Sisyphus" by Albert Camus: A Study Guide
"The Stranger" by Albert Camus: A Study Guide
"The Myth of Sisyphus" and "The Stranger" by Albert Camus: Two Study Guides *
Study Guide to "Death Comes to the Archbishop" by Willa Cather
"The Awakening" by Kate Chopin: A Study Guide
Study Guide to Seven Short Stories by Kate Chopin
Study Guide to "Ready Player One" by Ernest Cline
Study Guide to "Disgrace" by J. M. Coetzee
"The Meursault Investigation" by Kamel Daoud: A Study Guide
Study Guide on "Great Expectations" by Charles Dickens*
"The Sign of Four" by Sir Arthur Conan Doyle: A Study Guide *
Study Guide to "Manhattan Beach" by Jennifer Egan
"The Wasteland, Prufrock and Poems" by T.S. Eliot: A Study Guide
Study Guide on "Birdsong" by Sebastian Faulks*

"Oedipus Rex" by Sophocles: A Study Guide
"Cannery Row" by John Steinbeck: A Study Guide
"East of Eden" by John Steinbeck: A Study Guide
"The Grapes of Wrath" by John Steinbeck: A Study Guide
"Of Mice and Men" by John Steinbeck: A Study Guide*
"The Goldfinch" by Donna Tartt: A Study Guide
Study Guide to "The Hate U Give" by Angie Thomas
"Walden; or, Life in the Woods" by Henry David Thoreau: A Study Guide
Study Guide to "Cat's Cradle" by Kurt Vonnegut
"The Bridge of San Luis Rey" by Thornton Wilder: A Study Guide *
Study Guide on "The Book Thief" by Markus Zusak

Study Guides available *only* as e-books:
Study Guide on "Cross Creek" by Marjorie Kinnan Rawlings.
Study Guide on "Heart of Darkness" by Joseph Conrad:
Study Guide on "The Mill on the Floss" by George Eliot
Study Guide on "Lord of the Flies" by William Golding
Study Guide on "Nineteen Eighty-Four" by George Orwell
Study Guide on "Henry IV Part 2" by William Shakespeare
Study Guide on "Julius Caesar" by William Shakespeare
Study Guide on "The Pearl" by John Steinbeck
Study Guide on "Slaughterhouse-Five" by Kurt Vonnegut

New titles are added regularly.

Readers' Guides

Readers' Guides offer an introduction to important aspects of the text and questions for personal reflection and/or discussion. Guides are written for individual readers who wish to explore texts in depth and for members of Reading Circles who wish to make their discussions of texts more productive.

A Reader's Guide to Becoming by Michelle Obama
A Reader's Guide to Educated: A Memoir by Tara Westover

Made in the USA
Las Vegas, NV
05 August 2023

75690246R00042